Explore Our World

National Geographic

WORKBOOK 3

Series Editors
Joan Kang Shin
JoAnn (Jodi) Crandall

Authors
Lesley Ito, Jill Florent,
and Diane Pinkley

National Geographic Learning | Cengage Learning

Australia • Brazil • Japan • Korea • Mexico • Singapore • Spain • United Kingdom • United States

Unit 0

1 **Listen and read.** Match the questions to the answers. Draw lines. **TR: 2**

1. How do you spell *eraser*?
2. What's the difference between *on* and *in*?
3. How do you say *lápiz* in English?
4. I don't understand. Can you help me, please?
5. Could you repeat that, please?

a. I can show you.

b. Yes, sure.

c. It's a *pencil.*

d. e-r-a-s-e-r

e. Sure, e-r-a-s-e-r.

2 **Listen and circle.** **TR: 3**

1. 27 + 20 =	27 - 20 =
2. 101 + 35 =	101 - 35 =
3. 1,000,000	1,000,000,000
4. 1,000,000,000	1,000,000
5. 17th	7th
6. 2nd	3rd

3 **Do the puzzle.** Unscramble the words. Write one letter in each square.

Seasons and Months

Word	1	2	3	4	5	6	7	8	9
UMESMR					2				
WNTIER	1			8					
REBTOCO	9	13		10		7			
RUFREYBA					11				
PRNIGS	16		12						
TESBPMEER	17					6			
CAHMR		15		4					
BENREOVM		5							
LFAL			3	14					

4 **Find and write.** Look at Activity 3. Find the letters above the numbers. Write the letters above the same numbers in the squares below. Then read the message.

W																	
1	2	3	4	5	6	7	8	9	10	11	12	13	14	15	16	17	!

5 **Look, read, and write.** Use words from the box.

hers	his	mine	ours	yours	theirs

1
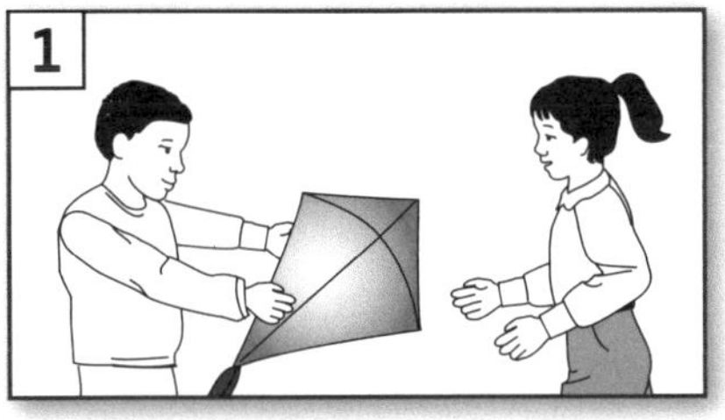

2

3

4

1. The kite is ______.

3. The kite is ______.

2. The kite is ______.

4. The kite is ______.

6 **Read.** Circle the correct answer.

1. Where's my hat? Oh, I see ___!
   a. me b. it c. them
2. Where's my sister? I can't see ___.
   a. you b. him c. her
3. I want a cookie. Can you give ___ a cookie, please?
   a. me b. us c. them
4. I like my friends. I like to play with ___.
   a. you b. me c. them
5. Do you see my brother? I can't see ___.
   a. you b. him c. her
6. Hello, Alex and Maria! I have cookies for ___.
   a. them b. you c. it
7. My friends and I want to play a board game. You can play with ___!
   a. us b. them c. you

Unit 1

The World of Work

1 Look and write.

a bus driver	a chef
a doctor	a farmer
a firefighter	a nurse
a police officer	a scientist
a vet	

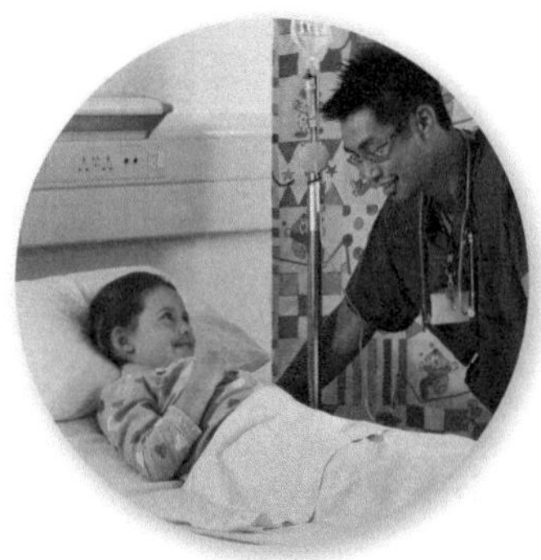

GRAMMAR

What **does** your sister **do**?	She's a vet.
What **does** his uncle **do**?	He's a firefighter.
What **do** your parents **do**?	They're scientists.
Where **do** your parents **work**?	They **work** in a lab.
Where **does** her brother **work**?	He **works** in a school.
Where **does** your sister **work**?	She **works** in a hospital.

2 **Read.** Look at the pictures. Write.

1. What ____does____ your cousin ____do____? She's a ____doctor____.
2. What ________ your grandpa ________? He's a ________.
3. What ________ your grandma ________? She's a ________.
4. Where ________ your aunt ________? She ________ in an animal hospital.
5. Where ________ your brother ________? He ________ on a farm.

3 **Read and match.** Draw lines.

1. Who helps you at school? — b
2. Who sings to people?
3. Who plays soccer?
4. Who is in the movies?
5. Who makes new things?
6. Who draws and paints pictures?

a. a soccer player
b. a teacher
c. an artist
d. an inventor
e. a rock star
f. a movie star

4 **Unscramble the words.** Write.

1. ferifihgetr firefighter

2. creocs arlyep ______________

3. viotnnre ______________

4. bsu direvr ______________

5. voemi arst ______________

6. sratti ______________

7. plocie ocfiefr ______________

8. okrc atsr ______________

GRAMMAR

What **do** you **want to be**? I **want to be** a police officer.

What **does** your sister **want to be** one day? She **wants to be** a scientist.

What **do** your cousins **want to be**? They **want to be** movie stars.

5 Listen and write. TR: 4

1. What ____________________ your brother want to be?
2. He ____________________ an artist.
3. What do your sisters ____________________?
4. They ____________________ inventors.
5. What ____________________ you want to be one day?
6. I ____________________ a rock star.

6 Look, read, and write.

1. He likes animals. What does he want to be?

   He ____________________.

2. She likes to work in the sun. What does she want to be?

   She ____________________.

3. She likes to play soccer. What does she want to be?

   She ____________________.

4. He likes school. What does he want to be?

   He ____________________.

7 Read and write.

1. Where does the teacher work?

   She ________________________________.

2. Where does the chef work?

   He ________________________________.

3. What does he want to be?

   He ________________________________.

4. What does she want to be?

   She ________________________________.

8 **Do the puzzle.** Read. Write.

1. This person works on a farm.
2. This person works in a hospital.
3. This person works with animals.
4. This person works in a lab.
5. This person works in a kitchen.
6. This person works in a hospital, too.
7. This person draws and paints pictures.
8. This person works in a school.
9. This person makes new things.
10. What does this person do?

    This person is a ________________.

9 **Listen and read.** Can you say these fast? TR: 5

1. My father's a fine fast firefighter.
2. Susie Silver sings seven sad songs.
3. The bus driver drives a big brown bus.

10 **Listen to the song.** Write new verses. Use words from the box. **TR: 6**

aunt	a bus driver
cousin	a firefighter
grandfather	a nurse
grandmother	a police officer
sister	a scientist
uncle	a vet

What does your ________________ do?

He's ________________. He's ________________.

He's ________________. Yes, he is!

What does your ________________ do?

She's ________________. She's ________________.

She's ________________. Yes, she is!

11 **Listen.** Which words have **f** that sounds like the **f** in **f**armer? Check the boxes. **TR: 7**

 ☐

 ☐

 ☐

 ☐

 ☐

12 **Say the words.** How many times do you hear **f** as in **f**armer?

Write. ________________

fly foot friends frowning grandfather
police officer phone sofa

13 Listen and read. TR: 8

The Dog Whisperer

Cesar Millan helps dogs. Some dogs have problems. They are angry or scared. Some dogs bite. People call Cesar Millan the "Dog Whisperer" because he teaches bad dogs how to be good.

Cesar knows what dogs like and need. Dogs need a leader. They need to have rules. Dogs need exercise, too. Cesar likes to run with the dogs.

The dog is Cesar's favorite animal. Cesar loves his job!

weird but true Dogs can learn more than a hundred words. Some dogs understand as many words as a young child understands!

14 **Read.** Check **T** for *True* and **F** for *False*.

1. Cesar Millan helps dogs. Ⓣ Ⓕ
2. Dogs do not need to run. Ⓣ Ⓕ
3. Cesar's favorite animal is the frog. Ⓣ Ⓕ
4. Cesar loves his job. Ⓣ Ⓕ

15 **Read.**

This is my Aunt Lily. She is a nurse. She loves her job. She works in a big hospital. At work she wears a blue and white uniform and black shoes. My aunt likes to help people. In her job at the hospital, she helps sick people every day.

16 **Write.** Write about a person you know. Write about his or her job.

1. Who is the person? ______________________________

2. What is the person's job?

____

3. Where does the person work?

____

4. What does the person wear?

____

5. What does the person do in his or her job?

____

17 **Write.** Put your sentences from Activity 16 together in a paragraph.

This is ______________________________

____

____

____

______________________________.

Unit 2

Let's Eat!

1 Look and write.

GRAMMAR

Are there **any** potatoes? No, there aren't **any** potatoes.

Are there **any** beans? Yes, there are.

Are there **any** bananas and mangoes? Yes, there are.

Is there **any** corn? No, there isn't **any** corn.

Is there **any** meat? Yes, there is.

2 **Listen.** Read and circle. **TR: 9**

1. No, there aren't any noodles.	Yes, there are.
2. No, there isn't any corn.	Yes, there is.
3. No, there isn't any ice cream.	Yes, there is.
4. No, there aren't any potatoes.	Yes, there are.
5. No, there aren't any tomatoes.	Yes, there are.

3 **Read.** Write the foods in the correct columns in the chart.

apples
~~bread~~
chicken
corn
eggs
fish
ice cream
mangoes
noodles
tomatoes

Is there any. . . ?	Are there any. . . ?
bread	

4 **Look and write.** Use words from the box.

cheese chips grapes nuts snacks yogurt

____

____

____

____

____

____

5 **Listen.** Read and write. **TR: 10**

1. Ken: Let's have a ______________________.

   Patty: ______________________________________ nuts?

   Ken: No, __________________________________. But there are some ______________________________.

   Patty: OK. ______________________________________ grapes.

2. Jill: I want a sandwich. ____________________________ cheese?

   Joe: No, ______________________________________. Sorry.

   Jill: Well, ____________________________________ chicken?

   Joe: Yes, _____________________________________. Here.

GRAMMAR

May I have some yogurt, please? Not right now. Dinner is at 6:00.

May we have some grapes, please? Yes. Sure.

6 **Write questions.** Write the words in the correct order.

1. have / cheese, / I / please / May / some / ?

   May I have some cheese, please?

2. some / we / May / milk, / have / please / ?

   ____

3. ice cream, / we / please / have / May / some / ?

   ____

4. I / have / chips, / May / some / please / ?

   ____

5. we / noodles, / have / please / some / May / ?

   ____

7 **Listen and write.** TR: 11

1. ______ I have some nuts, please? Yes. Sure.
2. ______ we have some bread, please? Not right now.
3. ______ we have some cheese, please? Yes, here you are.
4. ______ I have a snack, please? Not right now. Dinner is at eight.

8 **Play a game.** Start at **A**. Listen and draw a line when the answer is *yes*. **TR: 12**

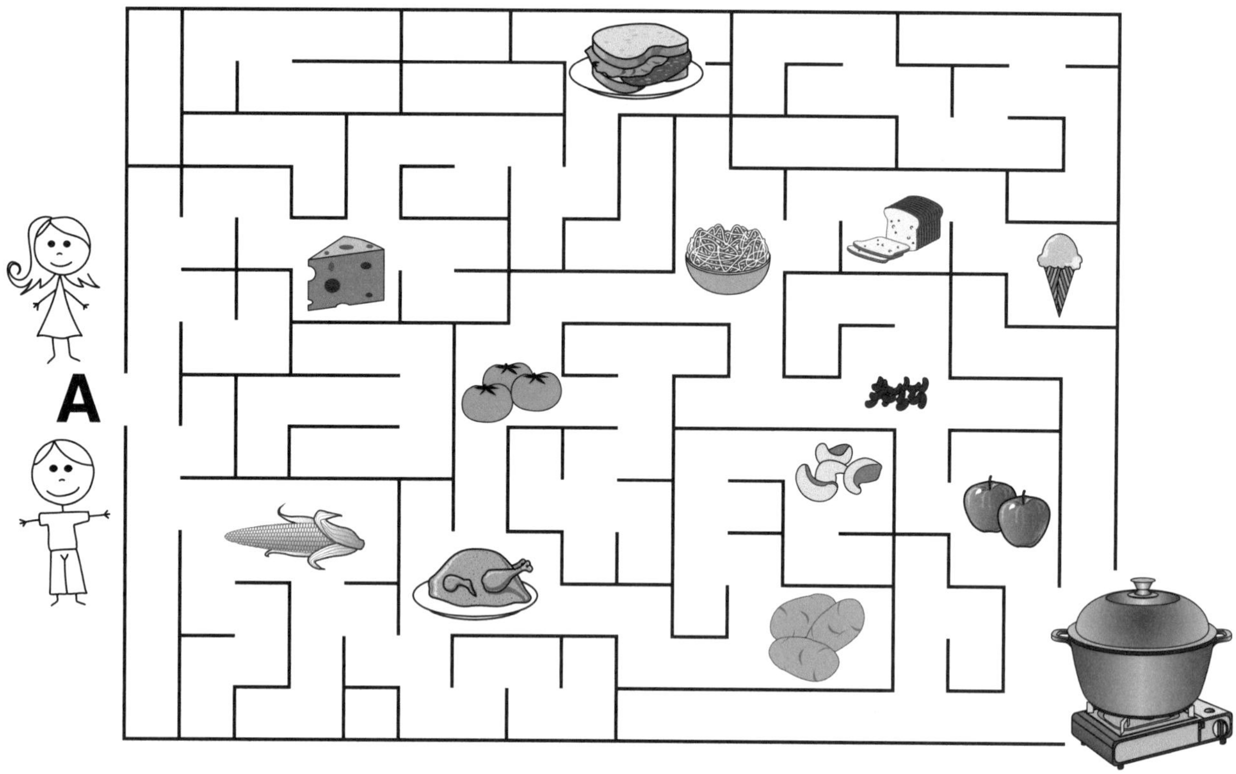

9 **Look at Activity 8.** What foods are there? Write.

I see ______________________________

____

____

10 **Listen and read.** Can you say these fast? **TR: 13**

1. Patty Peters likes peppers on her pizza.
2. Charlie's eating cheese with his chips.
3. May we have tomatoes, potatoes, noodles, and nuts?

11 **Listen to the song.** Write another verse. Use some words from the box. **TR: 14**

cookies	corn	noodles	potatoes
sandwich	soup	tomatoes	yogurt

I like ______________________.

And you like ______________________.

Let's make a ______________________!

12 **Listen.** Which words have **m** that sounds like the **m** in **m**ango? Circle, then color the pictures. **TR: 15**

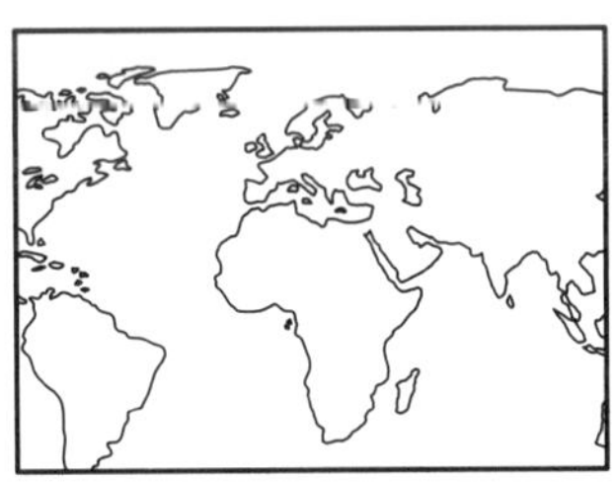

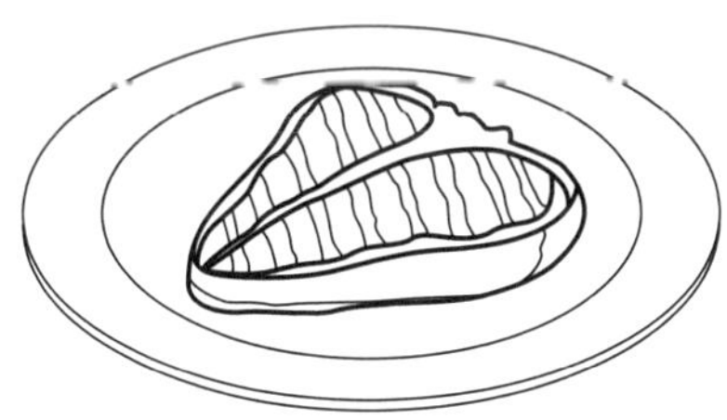

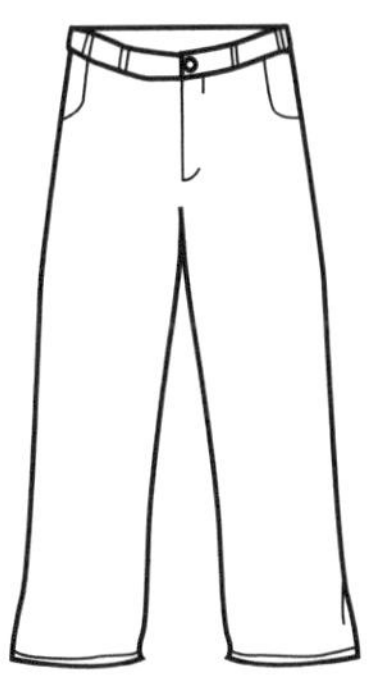

13 **Say the words.** How many times do you hear **m** as in **m**ango? Write. ______________

bedroom	climb	game	grandmother
lemonade	moon	mouth	umbrella

14 Listen and read. TR: 16

Super Foods!

Some foods help people be healthy. They are super foods!

Chicken, meat, fish, beans, eggs, and nuts are good for you. Brown rice and whole grains are good for you. Milk and foods made from milk are good for you, too.

Fruits and vegetables are great foods! There are fruits and vegetables of many colors. Eat a few different colors every day!

Candy and sugary foods taste good, but don't eat too much of them. Instead, eat super foods that can keep you strong and healthy.

weird but true **Some plants eat meat. They eat insects, frogs, and birds!**

Venus Fly Trap

15 **Read.** Check **T** for *True* and **F** for *False*.

1. Fish and nuts are good for you. Ⓣ Ⓕ
2. Milk and foods made from milk are good for you. Ⓣ Ⓕ
3. Fruits and vegetables aren't good for you. Ⓣ Ⓕ
4. Eat candy and sugary foods most of the time. Ⓣ Ⓕ

16 Read.

My Favorite Snacks

I eat my snack at home after school. I have lots of snacks I like to eat. Sometimes I eat fruits, nuts, yogurt, or cheese. Other times, I like to eat potato chips. And other times, I have a big cup of hot chocolate with cookies or bread and butter. But my favorite snack is a lettuce, mayonnaise, and peanut butter sandwich. Try it! It's delicious!

17 **Write.** Write about your favorite snacks.

1. When do you have a snack?

____

2. What are your favorite snacks?

____

3. How does your favorite snack taste?

____

18 **Write.** Put your sentences from Activity 17 together in a paragraph.

I eat ____

____

____

____

____ .

Unit 3

A Helping Hand

1 **Listen and write.** Then listen again. Read and match. TR: 17

carry	feed	help	hug
protect	take care of	teach	

1. I ________________ my grandmother. ☐
2. I ________________ my goldfish. ☐
3. An animal mother can ________________ her baby. ☐
4. I ________________ my mother. ☐
5. I ________________ the baby. ☐
6. I ________________ my brother the ABCs. ☐
7. I ________________ my bird. ☐

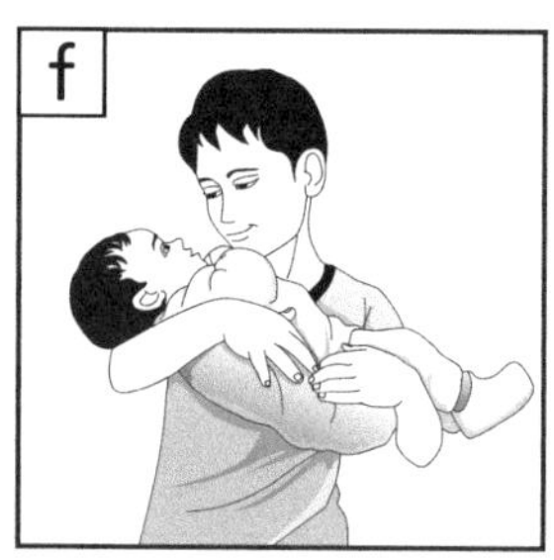

GRAMMAR

What does he do **before** breakfast?	He feeds his dog **before** breakfast.
What does he do **after** breakfast?	He brushes his teeth **after** breakfast.

2 **Unscramble.** Write.

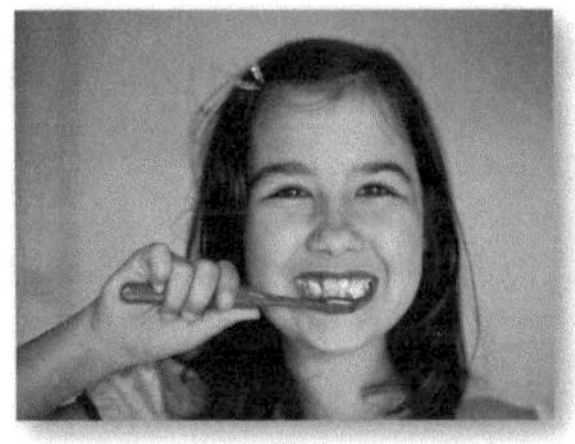

1. What does he do before school?
   washes / his / face. / He

   ____

2. does / after / What / do / he / school?

   ____

   He helps his mother.
3. breakfast? / What / do / before / she / does

   ____

   She brushes her teeth.
4. What does she do before school?
   feeds / hamster. / her / She

   ____

3 **Listen.** Match. Draw lines. **TR: 18**

1. What do you do after school?
2. What do you do before breakfast?
3. What do you do after breakfast?
4. What do you do before school?

a. I hug my grandmother.
b. I feed my cat.
c. I help my mother.
d. I take care of my brother.

4 Listen and write. TR: 19

come home do my homework have a snack make my bed take a shower

1. I ____________________ before breakfast.
2. I ____________________ after breakfast.
3. I ____________________ before dinner.
4. I ____________________ after school.
5. After my snack, I ____________________.

5 Look. Read and match. Write the number.

1. He takes a shower at seven thirty.
2. He makes his bed at eight o'clock.
3. He walks to school at eight fifteen.
4. He comes home at three forty-five.
5. He eats a snack at four o'clock.
6. He does his homework at four twenty.

6 Write.

When do you do your homework?

____.

GRAMMAR

	M	T	W	T	F
Omar **never** eats breakfast at 6:00.					
Omar **sometimes** eats breakfast at 6:30.		✓			✓
Omar **usually** eats breakfast at 7:00.	✓		✓	✓	
Omar **always** walks to school at 7:30.	✓	✓	✓	✓	✓

7 **Listen.** Draw lines to match. **TR: 20**

1. She	always	helps at home	at 3:15.
2. She	usually	has a snack	at 3:45.
3. He	usually	takes a shower	at 4:45.
4. She	sometimes	does her homework	at 5:30.
5. He	sometimes	makes his bed	at 6:30.
6. He	never	comes home	at 8:00.

8 **What about you?** Write about when you do things.

always
never
sometimes
usually

1. I ___always___ eat breakfast at ___7:00___.
2. I ____________ make my bed at ____________.
3. I ____________ eat lunch at ____________.
4. I ____________ have a snack at ____________.
5. I ____________ come home at ____________.
6. I ____________ do my homework at ____________.
7. I ____________ watch TV at ____________.
8. I ____________ go to bed at ____________.

9 **Do the puzzle.** Read the sentences. Unscramble the words.

1. 

It's four T W (E) N T Y (TTWYNE).
2. I ________ (LLSYAUU) drink milk for breakfast, but today I drank juice.
3. I ______ (SAAWYL) wake up early.
4. I _____ (NEEVR) get to school late. I'm always on time.
5. 

It's eleven ______ (RIYTHT).
6. He _____ (SAEKT) a shower in the morning.
7. I never eat a _____ (KCSAN) after school.
8. I brush my teeth _____ (REATF) breakfast.
9. I _______ (PERTOTC) my pet from wild animals.

10 **Answer the riddle.** Unscramble the circled letters in the puzzle to solve the riddle.

This animal is gray and has a long trunk. It's very big and can live to be seventy years old. African ones have big ears, and Asian ones have smaller ears. What animal is it?

(E) ( ) ( ) ( ) ( ) ( ) ( ) ( )

11 **Listen and read.** Can you say these fast? **TR: 21**

1. I slurp soup and sodas at six sixteen.
2. Meena makes many milk shakes in the morning.
3. Before four, fix the fifteenth flower vase.

12 **Listen to the song.** Read and underline. TR: 22

1. I have to comb my **cat / bird**.
2. I have to feed my **dog / snake**.
3. I have to pick up my **dog / frog**.
4. I have to wash my **goat / goldfish**.
5. I have to read to my **sister / brother**.
6. I have to teach my **sisters / brothers** their 1, 2, 3's.
7. I have to carry my family's new **baby / horse**.

13 **Listen.** Which words have a sound like the **o** in h**o**me? Draw a line to connect the pictures. TR: 23

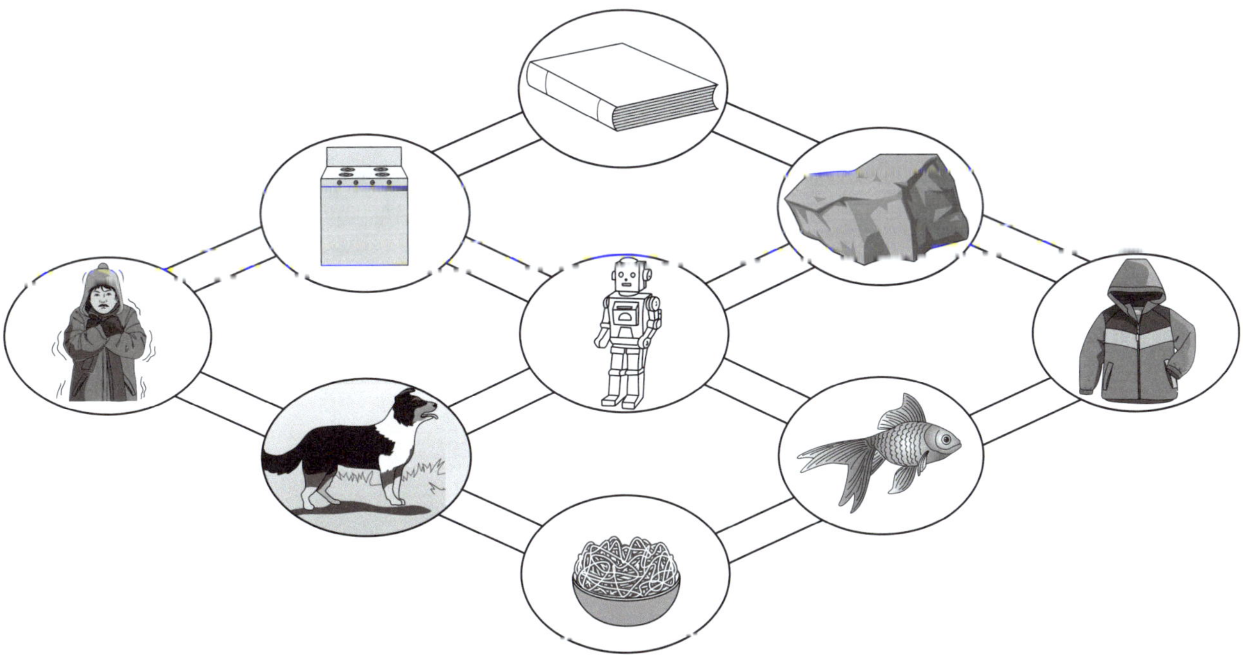

14 **Say the words.** How many times do you hear **o** as in h**o**me? Write. ____________

computer goat hippo notebook phone tomato yellow yogurt

15 **Listen and read.** TR: 24

The Daily Lives of Animals

People and animals usually live in different ways. They eat, sleep, and take care of babies differently.

The koala lives in Australia. It only eats eucalyptus tree leaves at night. The koala sleeps in the morning, afternoon, and evening. It sleeps more than fifteen hours a day! It has a small baby that grows in its mother's pouch.

The great white shark lives in oceans all over the world. The great white shark never stops swimming. It always eats and never sleeps. The mother doesn't take care of its babies. The babies swim away from their hungry mother!

Koala

Great white shark

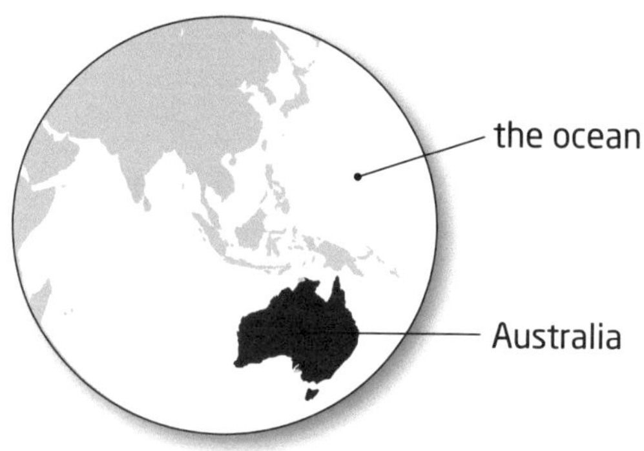

weird but true: **Many sharks are small. The smallest shark is the size of a man's hand!**

16 **Read.** Check **T** for *True* and **F** for *False*.

1. The koala sleeps more than fifteen hours a day. (T) (F)
2. The koala eats insects in the evening. (T) (F)
3. A great white shark takes care of her babies. (T) (F)
4. The great white shark always swims. (T) (F)

17 **Read the e-mail.** Naomi uses *before, after,* and *first* to show the order that her father does things. Underline these words.

Dear Carlos,

My father has a new job. He is a zookeeper! He takes care of the elephants. He gets up at 6:30. After breakfast he always goes to see the elephants. They are called Archie and Tina. He usually gives the elephants a bath first! He uses a lot of water. After that he feeds them. They eat lots of potatoes and carrots. Before lunch he cleans the elephant barn. Sometimes, in the afternoon, he walks with the elephants and helps them to exercise.

He loves his new job. I want to visit him at the zoo!

Naomi

18 **Write.** Think about someone who takes care of animals or people. What does this person do? When does this person do these things? How often? Write about his or her day.

____

____

____

____

____

Unit 4

My Place in the World

1 **Look and write.**

____

____

____

____

____

____

____

____

____

____

GRAMMAR

Can you **help** me? — Sure. **How can I help?**

Where's the museum? — It's **on** Main Street.

It's **next to** the police station.

It's **across from** the bakery.

It's **on the corner of** Main Street **and** First Street.

It's **behind** the movie theater.

It's **between** the park **and** the school.

2 Listen and match. TR: 25

1. Where's the supermarket? ___
2. Where's the toy store? ___
3. Where's the restaurant? ___
4. Where's the hospital? ___
5. Where's the bakery? ___

a. It's between the toy store and the park.

b. It's across from the bakery.

c. It's on the corner of Main Street and First Street.

d. It's behind the movie theater.

e. It's next to the museum.

3 Look at the pictures. Write.

Excuse me. ____________ you help me?

Sure. How ____________?

____________ the police station?

It's ____________ the ____________ and the ____________.

Thanks. And is there a ____________ near here?

Yes, it's ____________ the bakery.

4 Look and write.

a library   a mall   a stadium   a swimming pool   a zoo

____

____

____

____

____

5 Listen. Circle the answers. TR: 26

1. She wants to go to the **swimming pool / stadium**. She wants to **see her favorite baseball team / buy some shoes.**
2. I want to go to the **library / mall**. I want to **play in the water / study.**
3. He wants to go to the **zoo / mall**. He wants to **buy some new shoes / see the hippos**.
4. She wants to go to the **swimming pool / stadium**. She wants to **see her favorite baseball team / play in the water**.
5. I want to go to the **zoo / mall**. I love to see the **elephants / clothes**!

GRAMMAR

How can I get to the supermarket?

Go straight ↑.

Turn right → **on** White Street.

Turn left ← **on** Second Street.

6 **Look at the map.** Write.

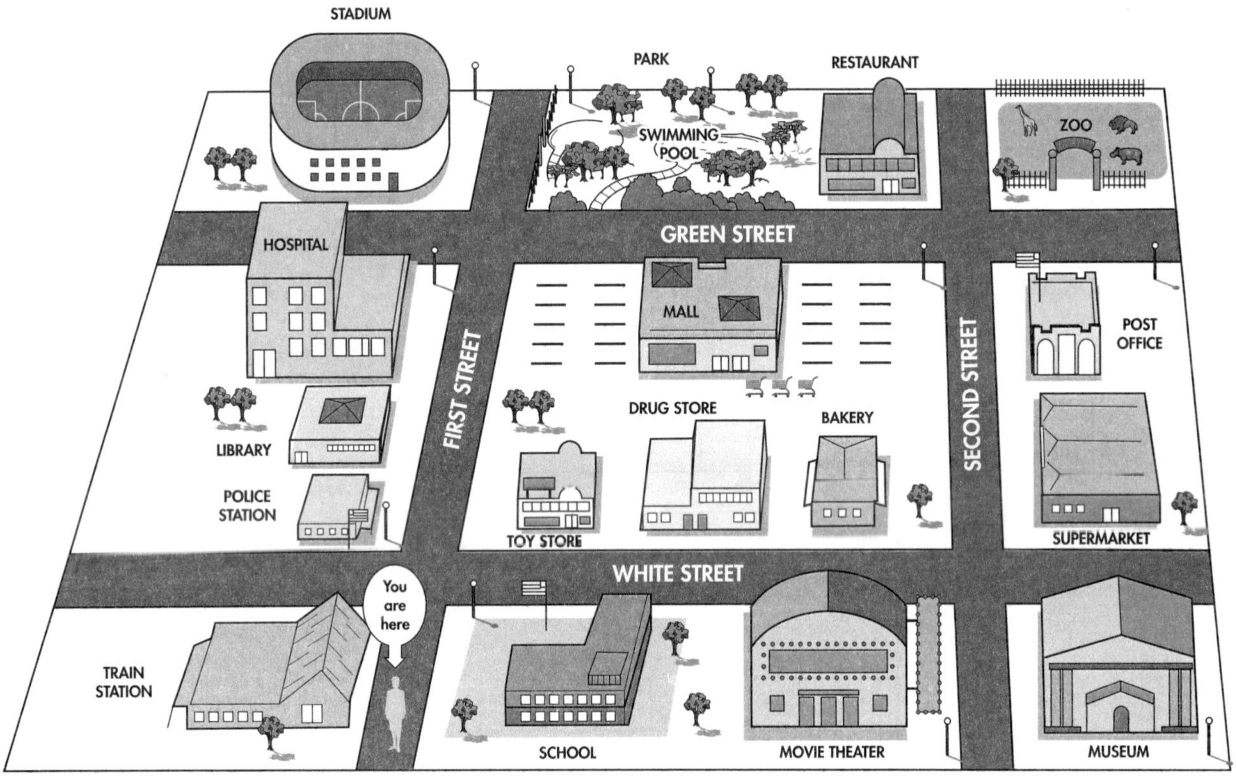

1. How can I get to the stadium?

   Go __________ on First Street. Turn __________ on Green Street. It's on the corner of ______________ and ______________.

2. How can I get to the bakery?

   Go __________ on First Street. Turn __________ on White Street.

   It's ______________ of ______________ and ______________.

   It's ______________ the movie theater.

7 **Read.** Do the crossword puzzle.

ACROSS

1. You can shop at many different stores here.
2. You can see soccer and other sports here.
3. You can jump in the water on a hot day here.
4. You can see doctors and nurses here.
5. You can buy bread, cakes, and pies here.
6. You can see many different animals here.
7. You can buy many kinds of toys here.

DOWN

8. You can see paintings and sculptures here.
9. You can learn English, math, and science here.
10. You can see police officers here.
11. You can buy meat, fruits, and vegetables here.
12. You can buy a ticket and watch movies here.
13. You can look at books and study here.
14. You can run and play or have a picnic here.

8 **Listen and read.** Can you say these fast? TR: 27

1. Six supermarkets sell salty shellfish.
2. Bill is busy at the bookstore buying big blue books.
3. Lisa is looking left for the library, but she's lost.

9 Listen to the song. Write a new verse. Write about your town. **TR: 28**

Where are the ______________________

and the ______________?

Where's the ______________?

Where's the ______________?

Where are the ______________________

and the ______________?

10 Listen. Which words have **u** that sounds like the **u** in m**u**seum? Circle the number. **TR: 29**

1. 

2. 

3. 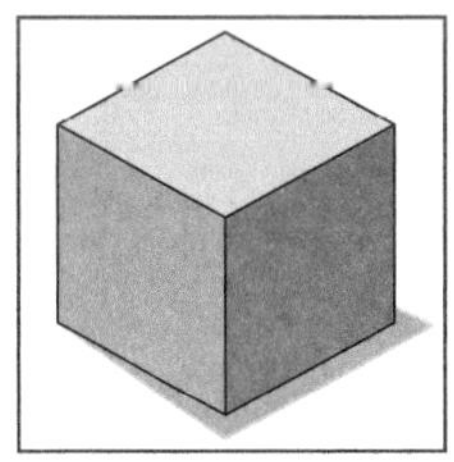

(4.) 

5. 

11 Say the words. How many times do you hear **u** as in m**u**seum? Write. ______________

community hug January jump menu stadium use you

12 Listen and read. TR: 30

A Town in Antarctica

The town of Villa las Estrellas is in the continent of Antarctica. Antarctica is very cold. People usually live there only for the summer, but some live all year round in Villa las Estrellas. About 150 people live there in summer. About seventy people live there in winter. Nights are long in winter. The sun shines only four or five hours a day. The sun always shines in summer.

Villa las Estrellas has houses, a bank, a school, a hospital, small stores, a post office, and a church. Many people come to visit. They like to go to the post office and send letters from Antarctica!

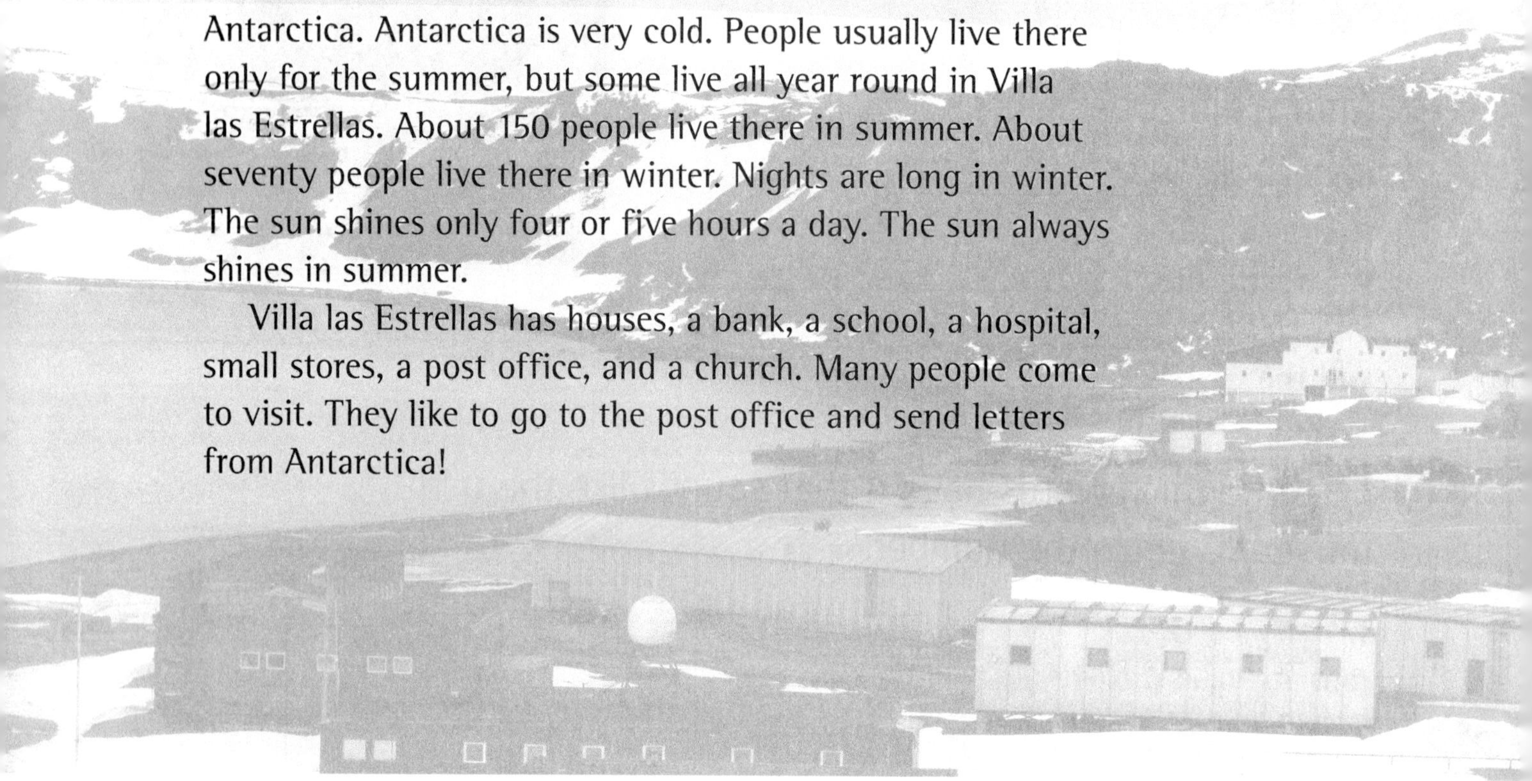

13 Complete the chart.

	Villa las Estrellas	Where You Live
Weather		
How many people		
Places		

14 **Read.** We can use the word *and* to connect two ideas. Underline the sentences with *and* as you read.

My Special Place in the World

My name is Jan, and I live in a town in Poland called Kazimierz Dolny. I have two favorite places!

There is a hill by the town. You can walk up the hill, and you can see the whole town. I think it's beautiful, and it's very quiet.

My second favorite place is the bakery! My town is famous for its special bread. The bakery makes bread in the shape of a chicken. It's delicious!

15 **Plan.** Think of a place that is special to you. Why is it special? How can you describe it? Fill in the chart.

My special place	
Why it is special	
Words to describe it	

16 **Write about your special place in the world.**

____

____

____

______________________________.

Review

1 Look and write.

1

2

3

4

5

1. What does she do? ______________________.
2. What does he do? ______________________.
3. What does she do? ______________________.
4. What does he do? ______________________.
5. What does she do? ______________________.

What do you want to be one day? ______________________.

2 Listen. Circle the answers. TR: 31

1. He **makes his bed / feeds his pet** before school.
2. What does he do **before / after** school?
3. He **sometimes / usually** helps his grandma.
4. I **always / never** do my homework at four forty-five.

3 **Look at the map.** Read. Write. Use some words from the box to complete the sentences.

across from	can	get to	go straight	help	how	left	next to	right

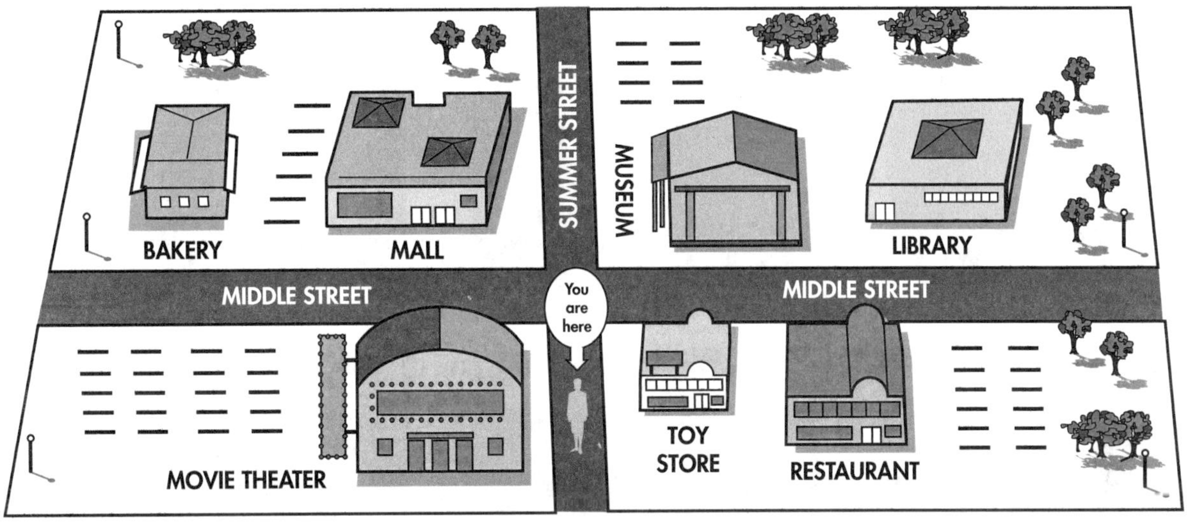

1. Excuse me. ________________ you help me?
2. Sure. How can I ________________?
3. How can I ________________ the bakery?
4. ________________________ on Summer Street. Turn ______________ on Middle Street. It's ________________ the mall.

4 **Write.** Use words from the box.

any	are	aren't	is	isn't	let's	there

1. I'm hungry. ________________ make sandwiches!
2. OK. ________________________ bread?
3. Yes, ________________________.
4. ________________________ any tomatoes?
5. Yes, ________________. There's cheese, too.

Unit 5

On the Move!

1 **Read.** Look at the pictures. Match. Write the letter.

a

b

c

d

e

f

g

h

i

1. a helicopter ☐
2. a boat ☐
3. a ship ☐
4. the subway ☐
5. a bus ☐
6. an airplane ☐
7. a scooter ☐
8. a taxi ☐
9. a motorcycle ☐

GRAMMAR

I ride my bike to the park.	**I do, too.**	**don't** = do not
I take the bus to the park.	**I don't.** I walk.	
My sister rides her scooter to the park.	My brother **does, too.**	**doesn't** = does not
My big brother rides his motorcycle to the park.	My sister **doesn't.**	

2 Read, look, and match.

1. Rodrigo rides his bike to the bakery.
   His brother does, too.

2. His mother takes a taxi to work.
   His father doesn't.
   He takes a bus.

3. My sister rides her scooter to school. I don't. I walk.

4. My grandfather takes the subway. I do, too.

3 What about you? Write a sentence with *do* or *don't*.

1. My friend walks to the museum. I do, too.
2. He rides a motorcycle to the library. I don't. I take a bus.
3. He takes the subway to school. I ______.
4. He walks to the park. I ______.

4 **Read and write.** Match the sentences to the pictures.

downhill   get off   get on   park   uphill

1. Sometimes I help my mother.

   I ________________ my bike,

   and I go to the bakery.

2. The bakery is at the top of a hill.

   I go ________________ to the bakery.

3. When I get to the bakery,

   I ________________ my bike.

4. I ________________ my bike

   next to the bakery.

5. After I go to the bakery,

   I ride ________________ to my home.

5 **Listen and check.** Check your answers to Activity 4. **TR: 32**

GRAMMAR

My sister takes a taxi to the mall, **but** my brother rides his bike.

6 **Read and write.** Read the sentences. Rewrite them using *but.*

1. My sister walks to school. My brother rides his bike to school.

   My sister walks to school, but my brother rides his bike to school.

2. I don't like to go uphill. I like to go downhill.

   ____

3. She walks to the movie theater. She takes a bus to the mall.

   ____

4. He eats snacks after school. He always eats his dinner.

   ____

5. A penguin can swim. It can't fly.

   ____

6. The girl is smiling. The boy is frowning.

   ____

7. My mother likes fruit. My father likes ice cream.

   ____

7 **Go through the maze.** Write.

1. I ride the ___bike___ to the ___scooter___.
2. I ride the ______ to the ______.
3. I take the ______ to the ______.
4. I ride the ______ to my ______.

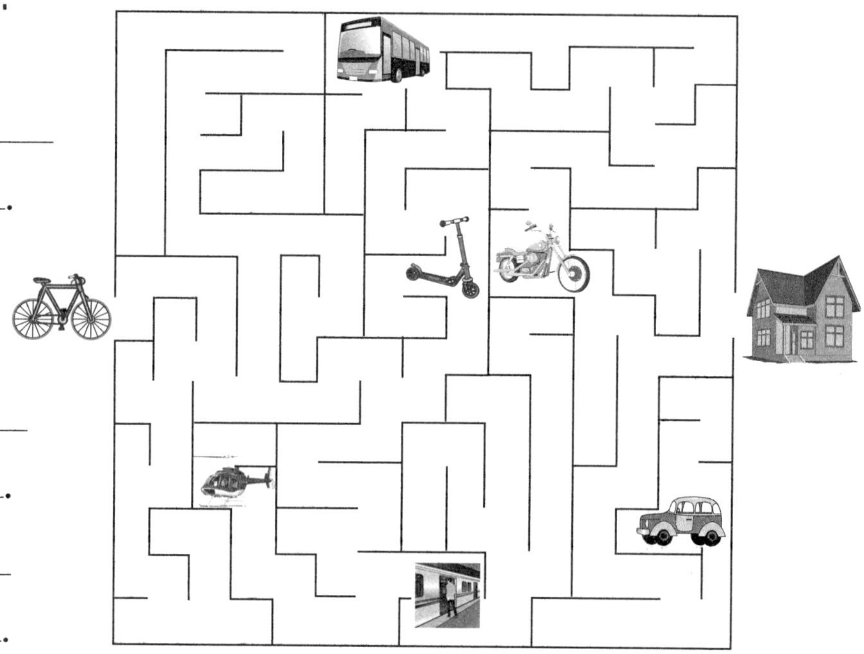

8 **Unscramble the words.** Write the words in the chart.

abot cetoyormlc hips linaprea pecilethor rosceot sub wusaby xait

Sky	Land	Water
	bus	

9 **Listen and read.** Can you say these fast? **TR: 33**

1. A motorcycle moves Mary to the mall on Monday.
2. Take a taxi to the tall tower tomorrow.
3. Six scooters scoot to the subway.

10 **Listen to the song.** Write a new verse. Use some words from the box. **TR: 34**

airplane helicopter horse motorcycle scooter taxi

I fly my ______________________ to school. Yes, I do.

I ride my ______________________ to school. Do you ride one, too?

I take a ______________________ to school. Yes, I do.

I take a ______________________ to school. Do you take one, too?

11 **Listen.** Draw an *X* over the words that don't have the same **oo** sound in sc**oo**ter. **TR: 35**

1.   

2.  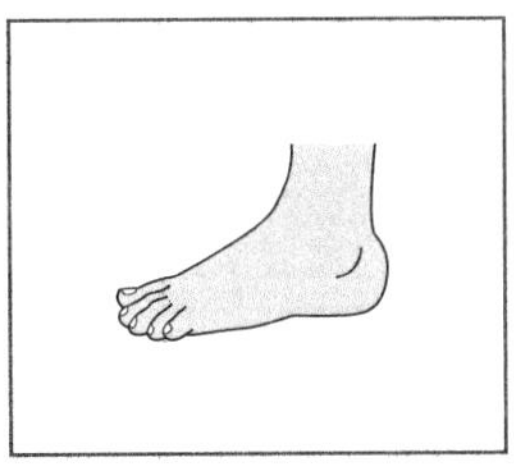 

3. 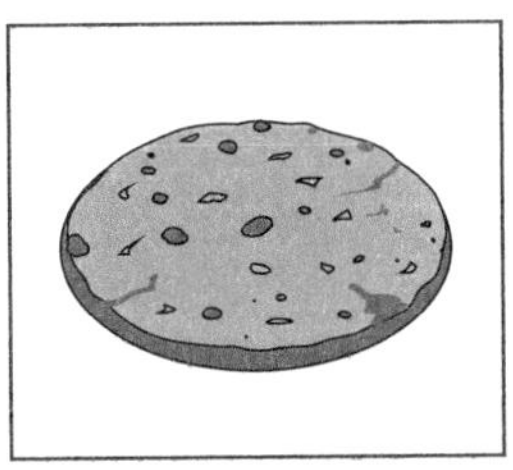  

12 **Say the words.** How many times do you hear **oo** as in sc**oo**ter? Write. ____________

bedroom food June moon notebook school shoe two

13 Listen and read. TR: 36

Going to School Is Cool

Many children take a school bus to school, but some children in India ride a special school boat! The children live on boats, but they go to school on land. They take the school boat in the morning.

Some children who live in the mountains of Colombia take a zip line to get to school. The zip line is long. The children aren't scared to take the zip line. It's fun!

India

weird but true

Fish don't go to school, but a group of fish is called a school!

Colombia
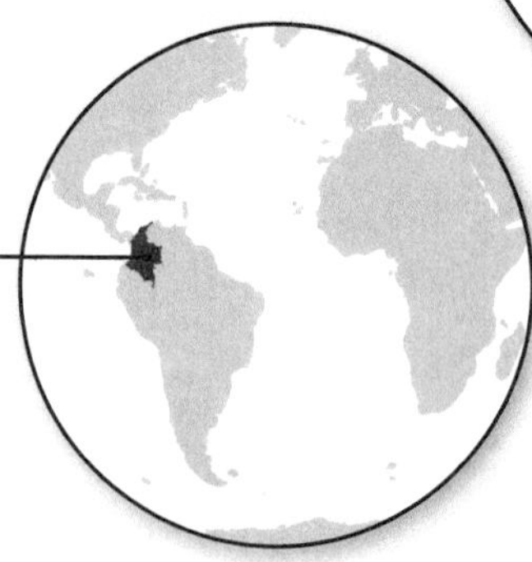

14 Read and write.

school boat zip line

1. In Colombia, some children take a ______________ to get to school.
2. Some children in India ride a ______________ to school.
3. What transportation would you like to take to school?

   I want to take a ______________ to school.

15 **Read.** We can use the word *but* to show that two connected ideas are different. Underline the sentences with the word *but* as you read.

Catch the Bus in Curitiba!

My city of Curitiba, Brazil, is famous for its bus system. It is called the BRT. There are more than a thousand buses in our city. There are many cars and trucks on the roads, but the buses use a special lane. They can move fast. In some parts of the city, you can catch a bus every 90 seconds. Many buses are typical size, but some of the buses are very long. They carry a lot of people. The buses are modern, and some of the bus stops are, too. At these stops, people can get on and off the bus in 15 seconds.

16 **Plan.** Think about your town. How do you usually go places? Describe how. Is it your favorite transportation? Why, or why not?

17 **Write.** Describe your favorite transportation where you live.

Unit 6

Our Senses

1 **Listen and look.** Write the number in the box. **TR: 37**

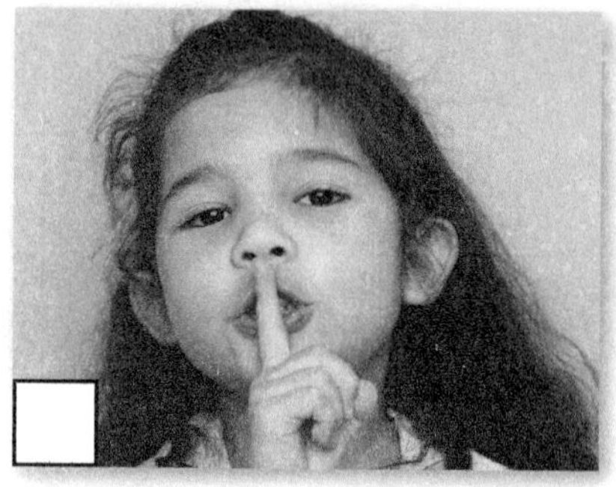

GRAMMAR

The cheese pizza **smells** great.
The dress **looks** beautiful.
How **does** the apple **taste**?
How **do** the teddy bears **feel**?

The helicopter **sounds** loud.
The cat **feels** soft.
It **tastes** delicious.
They **feel** soft.

2 **Read.** Check **T** for *True* and **F** for *False*.

1. The music sounds loud. (T) (F)
2. The flowers smell good. (T) (F)
3. The butterfly looks ugly. (T) (F)
4. The hamsters feel hard. (T) (F)
5. The sandwich tastes delicious. (T) (F)

3 Read and write.

1. How does the bread taste? It ________ good.
2. How ________ the sock smell? It ________ terrible!
3. How ________ the rocks feel? They ________ hard.
4. How ________ the dirty, old sneakers look? They ________ ugly.
5. How ________ the parrot sound? It ________ loud.

4 **Read and write.** Listen and check. TR: 38

bitter salty sour spicy sweet

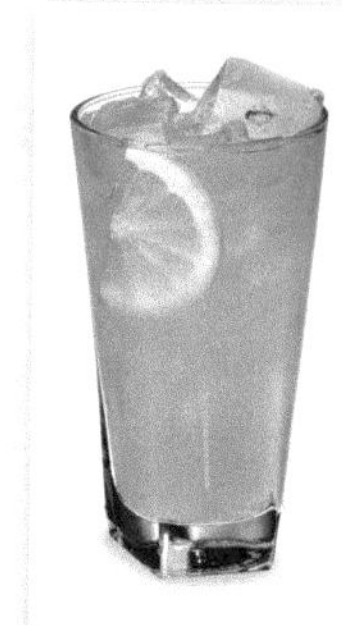

1. My mother drinks tea every morning,

   but I don't like it. It's ______.

2. Lemons are sour, but sometimes lemonade is ______.

peppers

3. There are peppers in the soup. It's very ______.

4. These chips are very ______.

5. This apple isn't sweet. It's ______.

5 **Read and write.** Sort the words. You can use words more than one time.

~~apples~~ bananas cheese chips coffee cookies lemons mangoes noodles nuts oranges soup peppers pizza tea yogurt

bitter	salty	sour	spicy	sweet
		apples		apples

GRAMMAR

How **is** the soup?	It**'s** good.
How **are** the cookies?	They**'re** good.
How **was** the bread?	It **was** good. More, please!
How **were** the cookies?	They **were** good. Can I have one more, please?

6 **Read.** Look and match. Write numbers.

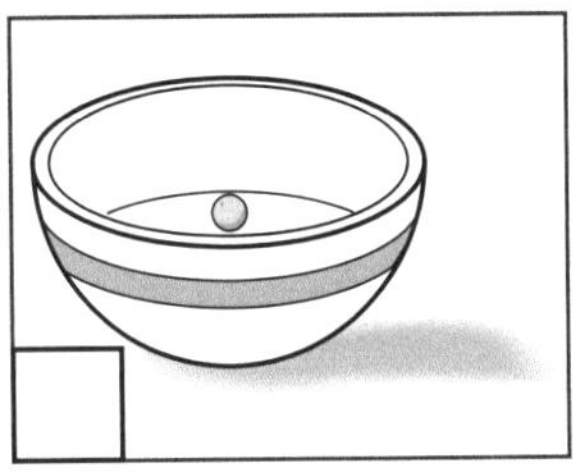

1. The bread is good.
2. The grapes are good.
3. The bread was good.
4. The grapes were good.

7 Read and write.

1. The soup ___was___ hot, but now it ___is___ cold.
2. How ________ the noodles? They were salty.
3. The baby ________ quiet, but now he's crying.
4. How was the ice cream? It ________ delicious!
5. The TV ________ loud, but now it ________ quiet here.
6. My little sister ________ sad, but now she ________ happy.
7. How were the tomatoes? They ________ sweet.
8. Her bedroom ________ blue, but now it ________ pink.

8 **Read.** Do the crossword puzzle.

Across

1. Flowers for me? Thank you! They're __________.
3. Your refrigerator smells __________. Clean it!
4. Please turn down the TV. It's so __________.
8. That painting isn't beautiful. It's __________.

Down

2. Lemons are sour, but lemonade is __________.
5. That chicken and rice smells __________.
6. Always be __________ in the library.
7. Don't eat the soup. It's very __________.

9 **Read and guess.** Write.

1. It's a fruit. It can be sweet or sour. It isn't red, and it isn't yellow. It's between red and yellow. What is it? ________________
2. It's a toy. It's soft. It can be any color, but usually it's brown. Some children sleep with it. What is it? ________________

10 **Listen and read.** Can you say these fast? **TR: 39**

1. Sonia eats sweet and sour ice cream on Sunday.
2. Bill buys big boxes of bitter brown beans.
3. Don't taste that terrible tea tomorrow.

11 **Listen to the song.** Draw lines to match. **TR: 40**

1. How does the cake taste?
2. How does a kitten feel?
3. How does the garden look?
4. How does a hug feel?
5. How does the drum sound?
6. How does a flower smell?

a. It smells good.
b. It feels great!
c. It feels soft.
d. It tastes sweet.
e. It looks beautiful.
f. It sounds loud.

12 **Write a new verse for the song!** Use some of the words from the box.

fire truck fish hard loud motorcycle quiet rabbit robot

How does a ____________________ feel? It feels ____________________.

How does a ____________________ sound? It sounds ____________________.

13 **Listen.** Which words have the sound of **s** as in **s**oft? Color the stars. **TR: 41**

14 **Say the words.** How many times do you hear **s** as in **s**oft? Write. __________

circle shoe desk shelf juice parents sock sofa

15 **Listen and read.** TR: 42

Stinky Animals and Plants

Many things smell good. But some animals and plants smell terrible!

The Eastern snake-necked turtle lives in Australia. If you catch one, it smells terrible. In Australia, people call this turtle the "stinker"!

Many flowers smell good, but the rafflesia doesn't. It smells terrible! The rafflesia is the biggest flower in the world. It grows in southeastern Asia. It smells like old meat. Flies like the smell, and they fly to the rafflesia flower.

a rafflesia flower

an Eastern snake-necked turtle

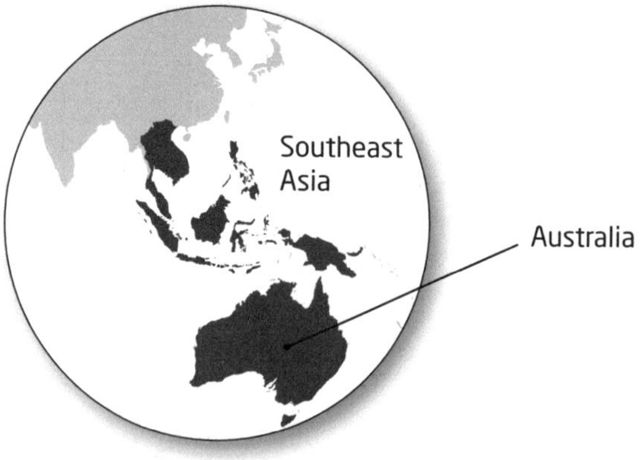

16 **Read.** Check **T** for *True* and **F** for *False*.

1. The rafflesia smells terrible. Ⓣ Ⓕ
2. The Eastern snake-necked turtle lives in Asia. Ⓣ Ⓕ
3. Flies like the smell of the rafflesia. Ⓣ Ⓕ
4. The Eastern snake-necked turtle never smells bad. Ⓣ Ⓕ
5. The rafflesia is a very big flower. Ⓣ Ⓕ

17 **Read.** We can use *and* to show that two connected ideas are similar. We can use *but* to show that two connected ideas are different. When we can choose between two connected ideas, we use *or.* Underline the sentences with *or.*

The summer is my favorite season. The weather is hot, and we do many activities outside. On weekends we visit our grandparents, or sometimes we go to the river with my cousins.

At my grandparents' house we sit outside and play cards, or we play with their pet dog, Charlie. My grandma loves flowers. They look beautiful and they smell great, too.

There is a river near my cousins' house, and we swim there sometimes. The water's cold, but I love it! We eat fruit, or sometimes we eat ice cream. My brother likes chocolate ice cream, but strawberry is my favorite!

18 **Write.** Write about your summer. Use *or* to show choices.

____

____

____

____

____

____

Unit 7

Animal Habitats

1 Look and match. Write the number.

1
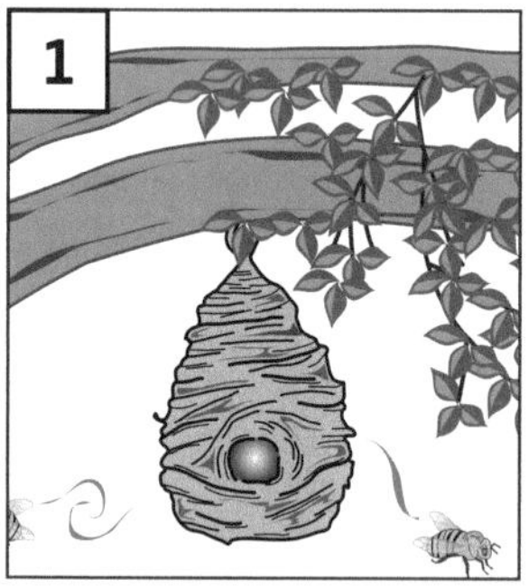

2

3
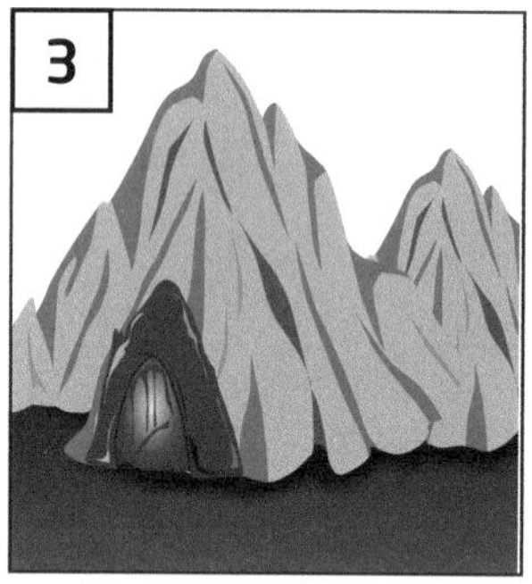

4

5

6

7
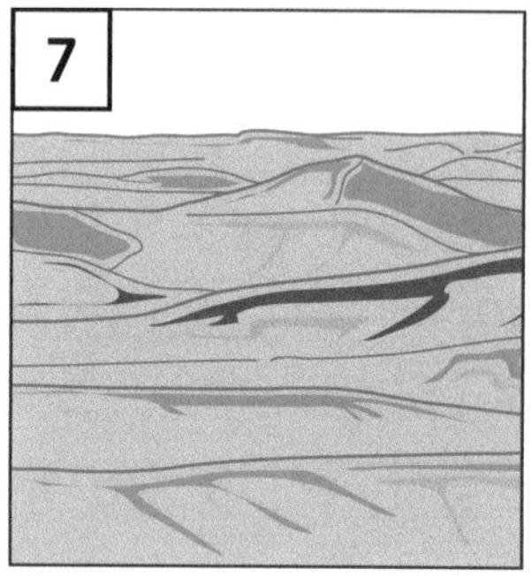

8

9

10
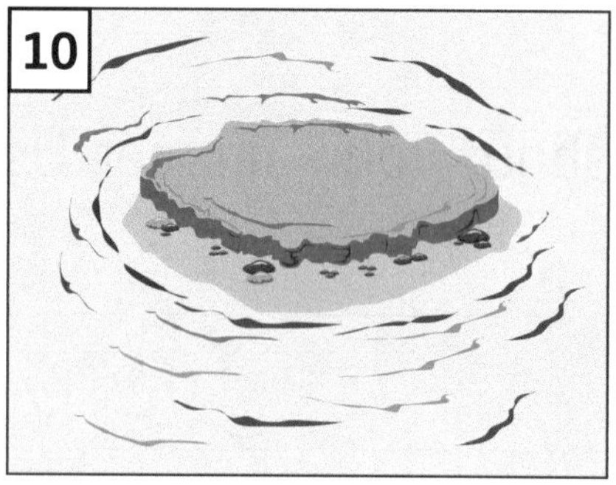

☐ ice	☐ a forest	☐ a desert	☐ an island	☐ a nest
☐ mud	☐ a hive	☐ snow	☐ a rain forest	☐ a cave

GRAMMAR

Why does a horse run fast? **Because** it has strong legs.

Why is the bear in the cave? **Because** the bear lives in the cave.

Why can frogs jump and hop? **Because** they have strong legs.

Why don't you like crocodiles? **Because** they are scary.

Why can't ducks climb trees? **Because** ducks don't have arms.

2 Read and write. Use words from the box.

are	Because	do	does	don't	is	Why

1. Why don't fish run?
   Because they don't have legs.

2. ______ hippos stand in water?
   ______ the sun is hot, and hippos feel cool in the water.

3. ______ the parrot eating a nut?
   ______ parrots like nuts.

4. ______ the desert dry?
   ______ there is very little rain in the desert.

5. ______ the birds by the water?
   ______ they eat frogs and fish, and frogs and fish live in the water.

6. ______ the tiger drink water?
   ______ it is thirsty.

7. ______ zebras live in caves?
   ______ zebras eat grass, and there isn't any grass in caves.

3 **Listen and write.** Use words from the box. TR: 43

fur	horns	pouch	tongue	wings

1. A kangaroo has a ______________.
2. A butterfly has ______________. It can fly.
3. A frog has a long, sticky ______________.
4. A goat has two ______________ on its head.
5. A lion has ______________.

4 **Look and read.** Check **T** for *True* and **F** for *False*.

1. A giraffe has a long tongue.	T	F
2. A cow has a pouch.	T	F
3. A chicken has wings.	T	F
4. A panda has black and white fur.	T	F
5. Some sheep have horns.	T	F
6. Many birds have colorful feathers.	T	F
7. Hippos have sharp claws.	T	F
8. Kangaroos have short tails.	T	F

GRAMMAR

Kangaroos use their pouches **to carry** their babies.

Parrots use their wings **to fly.**

Cats use their tongues **to clean** their fur.

5 Listen and write. TR: 44

to carry	to clean	to climb	to eat	to fight
to fly	to hide	to jump	to run	to swim

1. Goats use their horns <u>to fight</u>.
2. Polar bears use their white fur ______________ in the ice and snow.
3. Lions use their teeth ______________ meat.
4. Kangaroos use their legs ______________.
5. Ostriches use their legs ______________ fast.
6. Giraffes use their long tongues ______________ their ears.
7. Tigers use their mouths ______________ their babies.
8. Penguins use their wings ______________.
9. Cats use their sharp claws ______________ trees.
10. Owls use their wings ______________.

6 **What about you?** What do you use? Write.

1. What do you use to eat? ______________________________
2. What do you use to walk? ______________________________
3. What do you use to write? ______________________________
4. What do you use to carry things? ______________________________
5. What do you use to listen to music? ______________________________

7 **Read the clues.** Do the puzzle.

1. Why can a frog catch a fly with its ______? Because it is sticky.
2. Why can't a zebra fly? Because it doesn't have ______.
3. Goats use their ______ to fight.
4. Why does an owl have big eyes? ______ it needs to see at night.
5. Some bears live in ______.
6. ______ use a pouch to carry their babies.
7. Camels live in the ______.
8. Big spiders live in the ______.

1. GEONUT ☐☐☐☐☐☐ (2, 13)
2. GIWSN ☐☐☐☐☐ (3)
3. HONRS ☐☐☐☐☐ (12)
4. CEABESU ☐☐☐☐☐☐☐ (6, 5, 8)
5. VASEC ☐☐☐☐☐ (9)
6. NOKAGORAS ☐☐☐☐☐☐☐☐☐ (4, 10)
7. RETSED ☐☐☐☐☐☐ (7)
8. IRNA SROFTE ☐☐☐☐■☐☐☐☐☐☐ (1, 11)

☐ ☐ ☐ M ☐ L ☐   ☐ ☐ ☐   ☐ M ☐ Z ☐ ☐ ☐ !

1 2 3 4 5   6 7 8   9 10 11 12 13

8 **Listen and read.** Can you say these fast? **TR: 45**

1. My nephew never stands next to a nest.
2. We walk by the water in windy weather.
3. Do the polar bear and panda play in the park?

9 **Listen to the song.** Read. Draw lines to match. TR: 46

1. Why does a giraffe have a long, long neck?
2. Why does a frog have strong legs?
3. Why does a polar bear have white fur?

a. Because it lives in ice and snow.

b. Because it eats leaves at the tops of the trees.

c. Because it hops, swims, and jumps.

10 **Listen.** Which words have a sound like the **ou** in p**ou**ch? Draw a line to connect the pictures. TR: 47

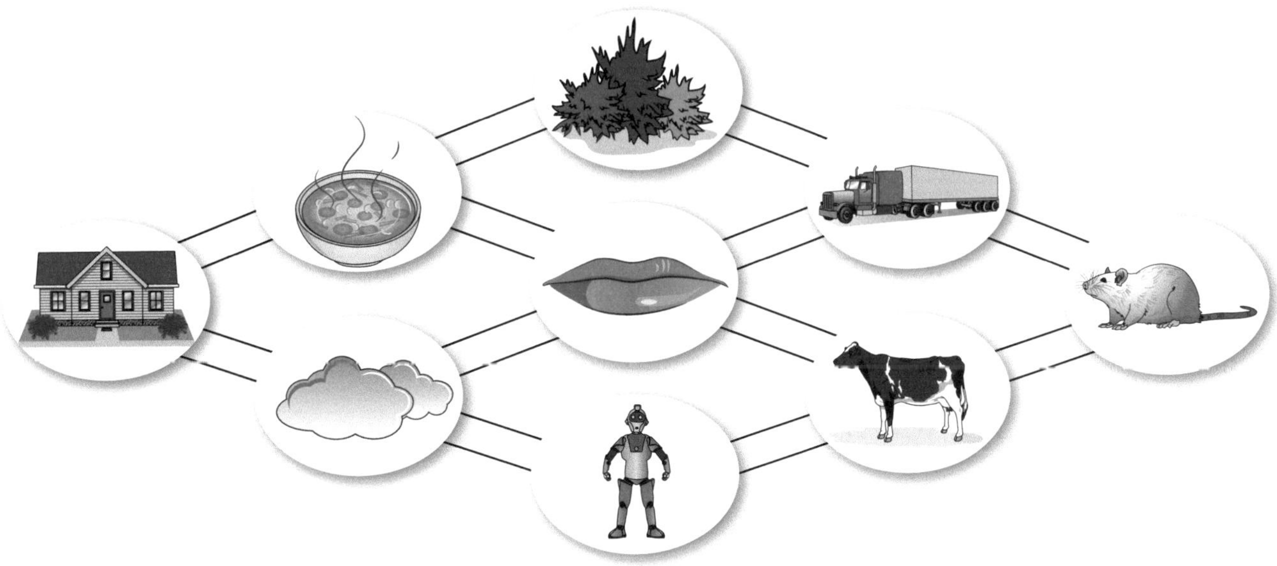

11 **Say the words.** How many times do you hear the **ou** sound you hear in p**ou**ch? Write. ______

brown clown count flower frowning sour yellow young

12 **Listen and read.** TR: 48

Animals in Antarctica

Antarctica is very cold, very dry, and very windy. Can animals live there? Yes, they can!

The emperor penguin is a bird. It can't fly, but it can swim. The mother penguin lays an egg on the ice. Where is the nest for this egg? The father emperor penguin takes care of the egg. He puts it on his feet! Why? Because he can keep the egg warm.

The Weddell seal lives in Antarctica, too. It spends a lot of time in the ocean. It can stay under water for forty-five minutes. The seal swims under the ice. Why? Because it catches fish and eats under water. It is safe under the ice.

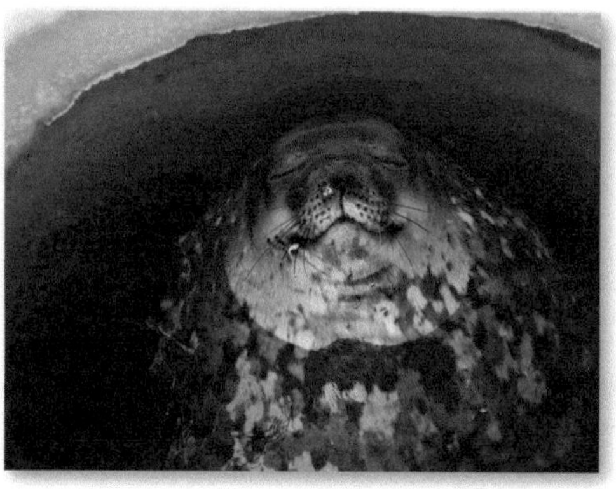

Weddell seal

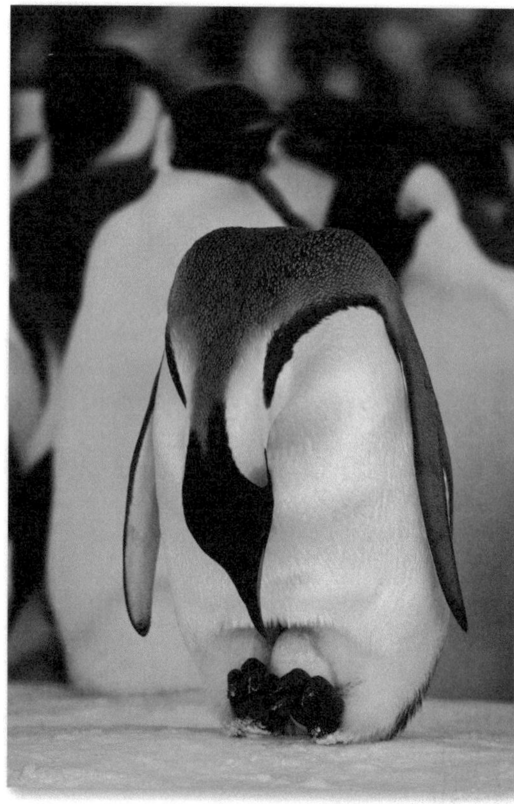

emperor penguin

13 **Read.** Check **T** for *True* and **F** for *False*.

1. The emperor penguin can swim well. (T) (F)
2. The emperor penguin father takes care of the egg. (T) (F)
3. The Weddell seal can swim under the ice. (T) (F)
4. The Weddell seal catches fish on the ice and snow. (T) (F)
5. Antarctica is hot and sunny. (T) (F)

14 **Read.** Read about Mounira's animal. Underline words that tell you what the animal looks like. Write the name of the animal.

My name is Mounira. I live by the Nile River. This animal lives here. What is it? Can you guess?

It lives in the river. It's brown and it has black spots on its back. It has four short legs and a long tail. It has big eyes on top of its head, and it uses them to see above the water. It has a strong mouth and sharp teeth! It can walk, and it can swim.

It is scary, but I like it!

Yes! It's a ________________.

hippo

turtle

crocodile

15 **Write.** Write about an animal you like.

____

____

____

____

____

____

Unit 8

What's for Dinner?

1 Listen and write. TR: 49

a bottle	a bowl	a box	a can
a glass	a jar	a loaf	a piece

a

b

c

d

e

f

g

h

1. ________________ of cake ☐
2. ________________ of sugar ☐
3. ________________ of oil ☐
4. ________________ of olives ☐
5. ________________ of soda ☐
6. ________________ of juice ☐
7. ________________ of cereal ☐
8. ________________ of bread ☐

GRAMMAR

Are there **any** boxes of cereal?	Yes, there are **some** on the table.
Are there **any** loaves of bread?	No, there aren't **any.**
Is there **any** cheese?	Yes, there is **some** in the fridge.
Is there **any** rice?	No, there isn't **any.**

2 **Listen.** Read and circle. **TR: 50**

1. Is there any cake?
   Yes, there is some.   No, there isn't any.
2. Are there any bottles of oil?
   Yes, there are some.   No, there aren't any.
3. Are there any pieces of cake?
   Yes, there are some.   No, there aren't any.
4. Is there any cereal?
   Yes, there is some.   No, there isn't any.

3 **Look at the picture.** Read and write.

1. Are there ___any___ beans?
   Yes, there are some in a jar.
2. Are there ________ cans of soda?
   ____
3. Is there ________ orange juice?
   ____
4. Are there ________ eggs?
   ____
5. Are there ________ bottles of apple juice?
   ____

4 **Listen and read.** Write. TR: 51

1. The __________ of that sandwich is five dollars.
2. Let's __________ the milk and eggs in the refrigerator.
3. I'm hungry. Let's go to the supermarket and __________ some food.
4. Which is better, yogurt or ice cream? Let's __________ them.
5. Oh, no! I don't have any __________! I can't take the bus home.

5 **Read and write.** Use words from the box.

buy compare money price put away

1. I'm thirsty. Let's __________ a can of soda.
2. The __________ of that bag of nuts is fifty cents.
3. I have twenty cents. Do you have any __________?
4. Which snack is better for me? I need to __________ them.
5. I __________ my toys after I play.

6 **Read and write.**

1. What is your favorite snack food? ______________________________
2. What is the price of your snack food? ______________________________
3. Do you buy it every day? ______________________________

GRAMMAR

Are there any olives?	Yes, there are **a few**.
Are there any apples?	Yes, there are **a few** in the bowl.
Is there any tea?	Yes, there is **a little**.
Is there any juice?	Yes, there is **a little** in the bottle.

7 **Read.** Write the foods in the correct columns in the chart.

~~apples~~	~~ice cream~~	loaves of bread	milk
oil	potatoes	sandwiches	soup

There are a few.	There is a little.
apples	ice cream

8 **Read and write.** Use *is a little* or *are a few.*

1. Are there any jars of olives? Yes, there ________________.
2. Are there any boxes of cereal? Yes, there ________________.
3. Is there any oil in the bottle? Yes, there ________________.
4. Is there any pasta in the bowl? Yes, there ________________.
5. Are there any cans of soda? Yes, there ________________.
6. Is there any sugar in the bowl? Yes, there ________________.
7. Is there any cake? Yes, there ________________.

9 **What's in your classroom?** Answer the questions. Write. Use sentences from the box.

Yes, there is some.	Yes, there are a few.	Yes, there is a little.
Yes, there are some.	No, there isn't any.	No, there aren't any.

1. Is there any water? ______________________
2. Are there any boxes? ______________________
3. Is there any soda? ______________________
4. Is there any glue? ______________________
5. Are there any snacks? ______________________
6. Are there any windows? ______________________

10 **Look at the pictures.** Circle the words.

h	k	d	p	r	i	c	e
c	s	x	y	q	g	p	a
m	o	z	c	w	t	p	j
q	a	m	z	x	s	w	b
e	f	v	p	b	g	t	u
p	u	t		a	w	a	y
y	j	m	i	k	r	l	u
o	p	l	m	o	n	e	y

11 **Listen and read.** Can you say these fast? **TR: 52**

1. Put away the pasta, peppers, and potatoes.
2. Betty buys a big box of bananas.
3. Compare the cheese, chips, and chicken carefully.

12 **Listen to the song.** Write. TR: 53

1. A jar of jelly is no fun,
   if there isn't any __________ to spread it on.
   __________ is very nice,
   but it tastes better with some spice.
2. __________, a jar of spice,
   __________, and __________ are nice!
   Let's go now. Let's buy some food.
   Let's go shopping, just me and you!

13 **Look at the pictures and say the words.** Write on the line the words with the sound of **j** that you hear in **j**uice.

____

14 **Listen and check your answers to Activity 13.** TR: 54

15 **Listen and read.** TR: 55

How People Eat

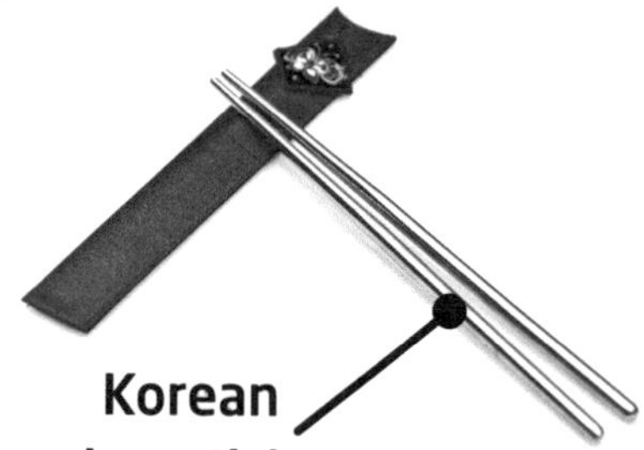

People eat in different ways. People in China, Japan, and Korea usually use chopsticks to eat. Chopsticks are different in each country.

People use chopsticks in Thailand and Cambodia, but they only use chopsticks to eat noodles. They use a spoon and fork to eat other foods.

People in Europe and the Americas usually use forks, knives, and spoons to eat. But people in India and Ethiopia use bread to pick up food. They eat with their right hand.

Weird but true: A chimpanzee uses a stick to eat ants.

16 **Read.** Check **T** for *True* and **F** for *False*.

1. All chopsticks look the same. Ⓣ Ⓕ
2. People in India eat with their right hand. Ⓣ Ⓕ
3. People in Cambodia always use chopsticks. Ⓣ Ⓕ
4. People in Europe usually use forks, knives, and spoons. Ⓣ Ⓕ

17 **Read.** Read this paragraph about Marcela's favorite meal. In a paragraph, the first sentence is called the *topic sentence.* It tells the main idea. The other sentences are called the *body* of the paragraph. They give more information about that idea.

My Favorite Meal

I love many kinds of food, but I have one favorite meal! First, I have chicken soup and some bread. It's delicious! I sometimes have two bowls! After that, I have fish cakes. I eat them with salad. Yum! And I have my favorite drink—apple juice. Finally, I have a piece of cake. So that's my favorite meal.

18 **Write.** Write about your favorite meal.

____

____

____

____

____

____

____

19 **Check your writing.** Circle *Yes* or *No.*

Does your first sentence tell what the paragraph is about? **Yes** **No**

Do the other sentences give more information about it? **Yes** **No**

Review

1 **Look at the photos.** Circle the words in the puzzle.

a	i	r	p	l	a	n	e	t	r	m
u	s	y	t	r	w	q	l	e	l	o
b	c	r	g	f	d	s	t	p	n	t
u	o	v	p	s	l	p	s	d	a	o
s	o	t	i	l	o	c	x	z	r	r
c	t	w	s	c	r	v	e	x	e	c
h	e	v	i	t	b	o	a	t	s	y
b	r	l	t	k	v	l	e	f	h	c
q	e	a	r	g	s	h	i	p	d	l
h	s	t	u	s	u	b	w	a	y	e

2 **Look.** Read and match. Write the letter.

a

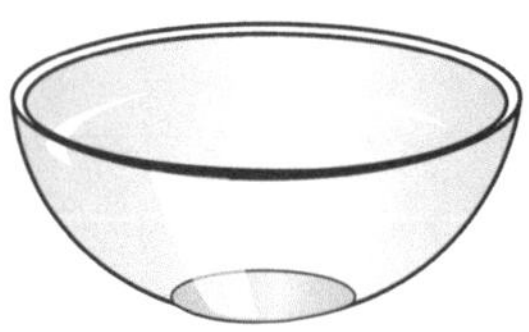
b

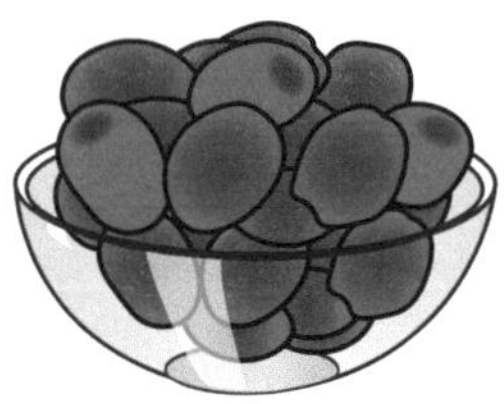
c

d

1. The olives are salty. ___
2. The cake was delicious. ___
3. The olives were salty. ___
4. The cake is delicious! ___

3 **Listen.** Read and circle. **TR: 56**

1. It sounds loud. It's very quiet.
2. It looks soft. It feels soft.
3. No, there aren't any. Yes, there are some.
4. Let's buy a loaf of bread. Let's put away the loaf of bread.
5. No, there isn't any. Yes, there is some in the bottle.
6. No, there aren't any. Yes, there are a few.

4 **Read and write.** Use some words from the box.

are	because	do	does	doesn't	don't	is	was	why

1. Why __________ lions eat bananas?
2. __________ lions eat meat.
3. How __________ the soda taste? It tastes sweet!
4. __________ does a zebra eat grass?
5. Why __________ the baby birds in the nest?
6. How __________ the soup? It was terrible!

5 **Read.** Check **T** for *True* and **F** for *False*.

1. A cat uses its tongue to drink. Ⓣ Ⓕ
2. A goat uses its horns to taste. Ⓣ Ⓕ
3. A parrot uses its wings to fly. Ⓣ Ⓕ

EXPLORE OUR WORLD

TR: 57

This is our world.
Everybody's got a song to sing.
Each boy and girl.
This is our world!

I say "our," you say "world."
Our!
World!
Our!
World!

I say "boy," you say "girl."
Boy!
Girl!
Boy!
Girl!

I say everybody move...
I say everybody stop...
everybody stop!

This is our world.
Everybody's got a song to sing.
Each boy and girl.
This is our world!

Unit 1 **Work** TR: 6

What does your father do?
What does your mother do?
What does your brother do?
What do they do?

What does your father do?

He's a doctor. He's a doctor.
He's a doctor. Yes, he is!

I want to be a doctor!
I want to be a singer!
I want to be a rock star!
I want to be a farmer!
I want to be a dentist!
I want to be a chef!
I want to do it all!

CHORUS

What does your mother do?

She's a singer. She's a singer.
She's a singer. Yes, she is!

CHORUS

What does your brother do?

He's a teacher. He's a teacher.
He's a teacher. Yes, he is.

What do you like to do?
What do you want to be?
What do you want to be?
Please tell me!

I want to be a doctor!
I want to be a singer!
I want to be a rock star!
I want to be a farmer!
I want to be a dentist!
I want to be a chef!
I want to do it all!

CHORUS

Unit 2 **Let's Eat!** TR: 14

Let's eat!
Do you like chicken?
Let's eat!
Do you like bread?
Let's eat!
Are there any carrots?
Let's eat!

Are there any mangoes?
Is there any cheese?
Is there any yogurt?
May I have some, please?

Yes, there are mangoes.
Yes, there is some cheese.
There isn't any yogurt.
Come and eat with me.

CHORUS

Is there any pasta?
Are there any beans?
Is there any meat?
May I have some, please?

Yes, there is some pasta.
Yes, there are beans.
There isn't any meat.
Please, come and eat
with me.

CHORUS

I like chicken.
And you like beans.
Let's make a soup!

CHORUS

Let's eat!

Unit 3 Taking Care TR: 22

I love taking care of my pets.
I love taking care of my family.
I love taking care of them all.
I'm happy that there are so many!

I love taking care of my pets.
I love to pick them up, and hug them, too.
But before I get to play with my pets,
I have some work to do.

I have to comb my cat, feed my dog,
protect my bird, and pick up my frog.
I have to wash my goat, brush my horse,
And I can't forget to bathe my snake, of course.

CHORUS

I love taking care of my family.
I love to hug them, too.
But before I get to play with my family,
I have some work to do.

I have to read to my sister,
take care of my brothers,
and hold hands with my grandmother.
I have to teach my brothers their 1, 2, 3's
and carry my family's new baby.

I love taking care of my pets.
I love taking care of my family.
After all my work is done,
I get to have some fun with my...
cat and dog, bird and frog,
goat and horse, and my snake, of course!
My sisters and my brothers, my grandmother,
and even my family's new baby!

Unit 4 A Great New Town TR: 28

Can I help you? You look lost.
Can I help you find your way?
Can I help you? You look lost.
Can I help you today?

I'm new in town. I think I'm lost.
Can you help me find my way?
I'm new in town.
Can you help me with my busy day?

Where are the post office, the toy store,
the supermarket, and the park?
Where's the bakery?
Where's the library?
Where are the zoo, the school, and a
swimming pool?

CHORUS

I can help you. You're not lost.
I can help you find your way.
I can help you. You're not lost.
I can help you today.

Here's the post office,

the toy store, the supermarket,
and the park.
Here's the bakery, the library, the zoo,
the school, a swimming pool,
and a movie theater, too!

I can help you. You're not lost.
I can help you today.
I can help you find your way, and you'll be OK,
in your great new town today!

Thank you for helping me to find my way.
Thank you for helping me with my busy day,
in my great new town today!
In my great new town today!

Unit 5 How Do You Get to School? TR: 34

How do you get to school?
How do you get to school?
How do you get to school?
How do you get to school?

I take the bus to school.
I do, too.
I ride my bike to school.
I do, too.

CHORUS

My mom drives me to school.
My mom does, too.
I coast downhill to school.
I do, too.

CHORUS

Listen and I'll tell you
Listen and I'll tell you
Listen and I'll tell you
how I get to school.

I take a ferry to school. Yes, I do.
I take a ferry to school. Do you take one, too?

I take the subway to school. Yes, I do.
I take the subway to school. Do you take it, too?

CHORUS

Unit 6 Our Senses TR: 40

How does the cake taste?
It tastes sweet.
How does a kitten feel?
It feels soft.

Let's count our senses, 1, 2, 3, 4, 5!
Listen.
Look.
Feel.
Taste.
Smell.
It's great to be alive!

How does the drum sound?
It sounds loud.
How does a flower smell?
It smells good.

CHORUS

How does the garden look?
It looks beautiful.
How does a hug feel?
It feels great!

CHORUS

Unit 7 **Why? Because** TR: 46

Why does a giraffe have a long, long neck?
Why?
Why?
Because it eats leaves at the tops of the trees.

I want to know why.
I want to know why.
Why?
Because I want to know why!

Why does a frog have strong legs?
Why?
Why?
Because it hops, swims, and jumps.

CHORUS

Animals are amazing.
They do so many things.
And I have just one thing to say.
Why?

Why does a polar bear have white fur?
Why?
Why?
Because it lives in ice and snow.

CHORUS

Unit 8 **Let's Go Shopping!** TR: 58

Let's go shopping. Let's go shopping,
let's go shopping today.
Let's go shopping to buy some food,
then go home to put it away.

A jar of jelly is no fun,
if there isn't any bread to spread it on.
A bowl of rice is very nice,
but it tastes better with some spice.

CHORUS

Let's buy some pasta at the shop,
and some sauce to put on top.
Let's buy a cake. Cake's a treat.
I like cake because it's sweet!

A bowl of pasta, a jar of spice,
a glass of milk, and cake are nice!
Let's go now. Let's buy some food.
Let's go shopping, just me and you!

CHORUS